There's so much Blue and her friends are learning in school!
Today they're learning about books and reading.
Miss Marigold asks everyone to choose a book to use while they learn.

Can you find **10** books?  them.

Miss Marigold points to the **big words** on the **cover** of her book.
"These words tell the **title** of the book," she says.
Blue wants to find the **title** of each book on the shelves.

Will you help her?  the **title** of each book.

WILD ANIMALS

DUCKS!

GOOD SNACKS!

PLANTS

FLOWERS

THREE LITTLE PIGS

NUMBERS
1 2 3

BOATS

THINGS THAT FLY

CARS AND TRUCKS

UNDER THE SEA

LEAVES

ALL ABOUT BIRDS

The picture on the cover of a book can tell you what the book is about. Periwinkle's book has a boat on the cover. What do you think his book is about?

  at each cover.  the book about bugs **red**.

 the book about planets **blue**.

ALL ABOUT ANTS

OUTER SPACE

Good book-looking!

Will you help Blue count the different kinds of books? Great!

 at each cover.

1-2-3 How many books are about fruit?   1   (2)   3

1-2-3 How many books are about dinosaurs?   1   2   3

1-2-3 How many books are about flowers?   1   2   3

Periwinkle loves books! He would like to write a storybook one day.

 the things Periwinkle could use to write a book.

BOATS

6

Magenta loves to draw pictures. She imagines drawing pictures for a book about fish. Will you help? Great!

 the fish Magenta drew.

Thanks for helping!

Purple Kangaroo points to the **words** in his book.
Orange Kitten points to the **pictures**.

 the parts of the pages

that have **words** **purple**.

 the parts of the pages that

have **pictures** orange.

A jet can fly very fast!

A sea plane lands on water.

at more pages from Purple Kangaroo's book.

 the parts of the pages that have **words**.

 a box around the parts of the pages that have **pictures**.

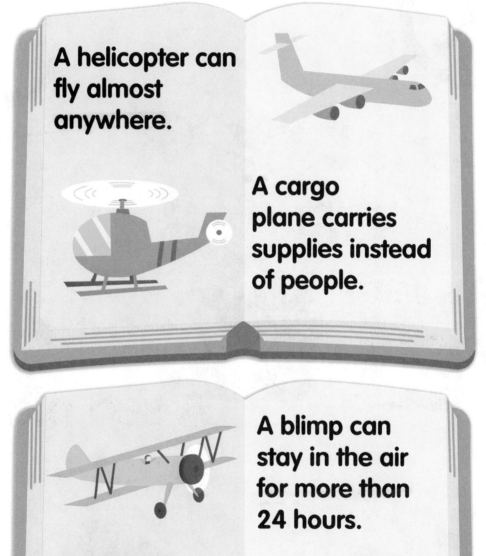

A helicopter can fly almost anywhere.

A cargo plane carries supplies instead of people.

A biplane has two main wings.

A blimp can stay in the air for more than 24 hours.

at Periwinkle's book.

 lines from Periwinkle's book to the pictures that could be inside of it.

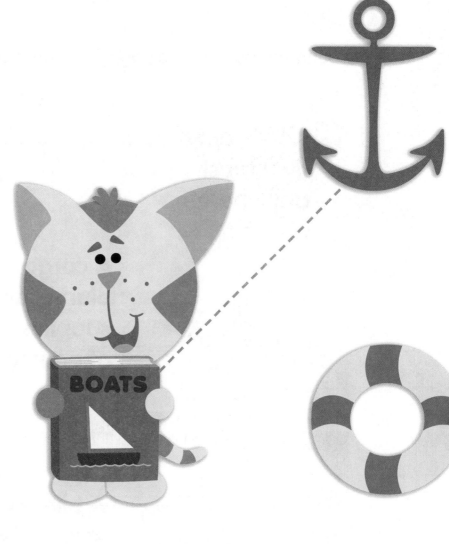

at Green Puppy's book.

Will you the pictures that might be inside Green Puppy's book?

CARS AND TRUCKS

READ123

Magenta knows that every story has a **beginning**, a **middle** and an **end**.

 at each picture from Magenta's book.

1 for the **beginning** picture.

2 for the **middle** picture.

3 for the **end**.

1   2   3   1   2   3   (1)   2   3

You found the beginning , middle and end—Good job!

lines to help Blue match each picture to its number order.

1
Beginning

2
Middle

3
End

at these pictures from Orange Kitten's book.

a number to put each picture in order from **1** to **4**.

1 2 3 4

1 2 3 4

1 2 3 4

1 2 3 4

Let's look at more pictures from Orange Kitten's book!

lines to put them in order from **1** to **4**.

1

2

3

4

15

At Circle Time, Blue picks a **left** arrow from the Learning Box. Magenta picks a **right** arrow.

Blue wants to play a **left** and **right** game.
"Good idea!" says Miss Marigold.
Will you play, too? Terrific!

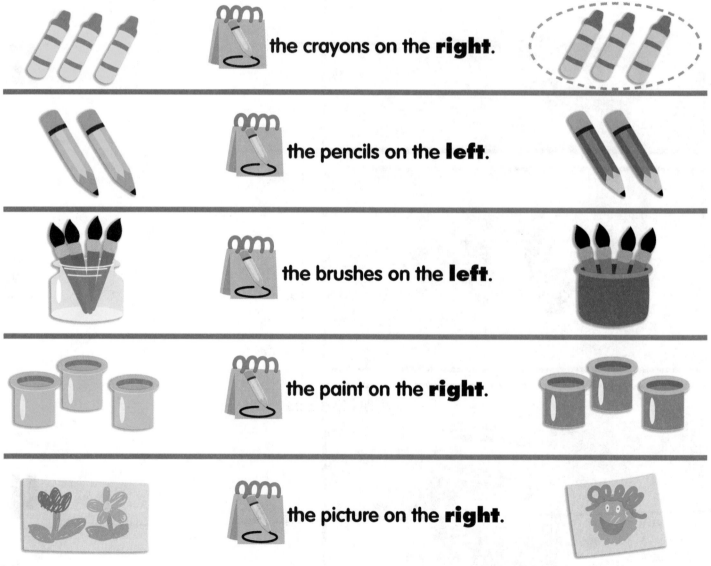

the crayons on the **right**.

the pencils on the **left**.

the brushes on the **left**.

the paint on the **right**.

the picture on the **right**.

Periwinkle wants to practice left and right, too.

  the **A** on the **left**.

   the **B** on the **right**.

   the **C** on the **right**.

  the **D** on the **left**.

  the **E** on the **right**.

  the **F** on the **left**.

  the **G** on the **right**.

Miss Marigold says that words are read from left to right.

a line from **left** to **right** from each friend to a toy.

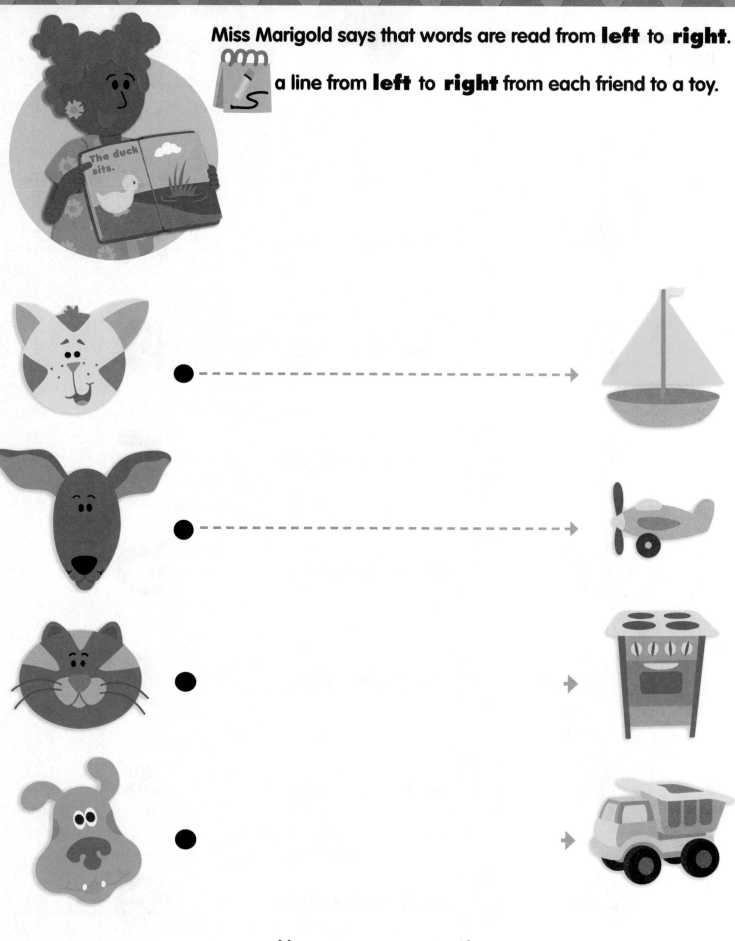

You sure are smart!

Will you help Magenta follow words from **left** to **right**? Great!

 a line under the words from the **blue** word to the red one.

The **plant is** green.

It **is in a** red pot.

The **plant likes** sun.

The **plant likes** water.

Grow, **plant,** grow!

Great job practicing left and right! Now let's practice **top** and **bottom**.

First, all the pictures at the **top** of the box.

Then all the words at the **bottom** of the box.

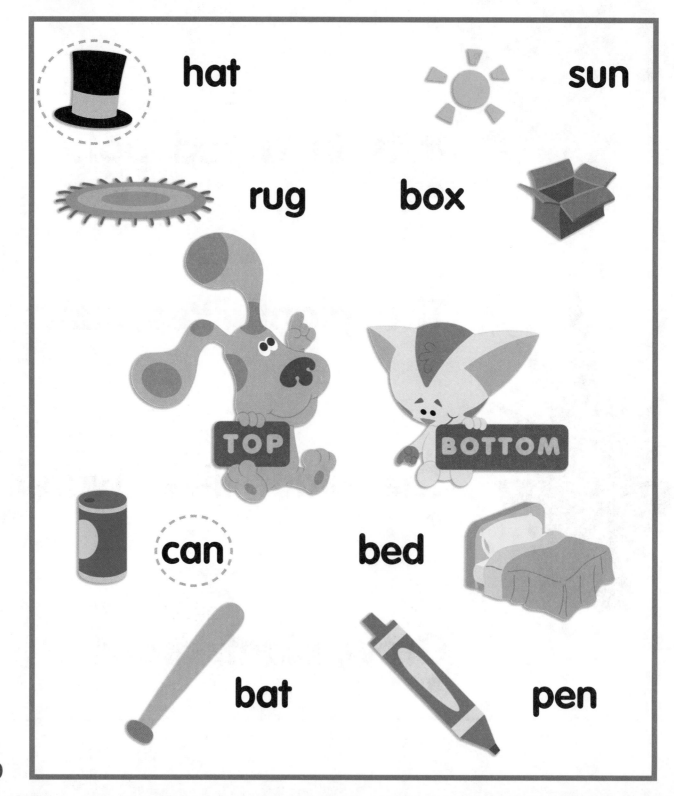

hat

sun

rug   box

TOP   BOTTOM

can   bed

bat   pen

Miss Marigold says pages are read from the **top** to the **bottom**.

 lines from **top** to **bottom**

to give each friend a snack.

Blue has practiced **left** to **right** and **top** to **bottom**.
It's time to put it all together to follow the words on a page.

Will you help Blue follow the words on a page?
Follow the number order from **1–10**.

lines under the words.

① **②** **③**

Mama   Duck   swims

④ **⑤** **⑥** **⑦**

in   the   pond.   Baby

⑧ **⑨** **⑩**

Duck   swims,   too.

lines under the words from **1-12**.

①   **②**   **③**

Mama   sees   a

- - - - - - - - - - - - - - - -

④   **⑤**

green   frog.

⑥   **⑦**   **⑧**

"Ribbut!" says Frog.

⑨   **⑩**   **⑪**   **⑫**

"Quack!" say the ducks.

Good word-following!

Periwinkle and Magenta know that words are made of letters.
Do you know all the letters of the alphabet?

ABCDEFGHIJKLMN

a line to connect the dots from **A** to **M**. Then the picture.

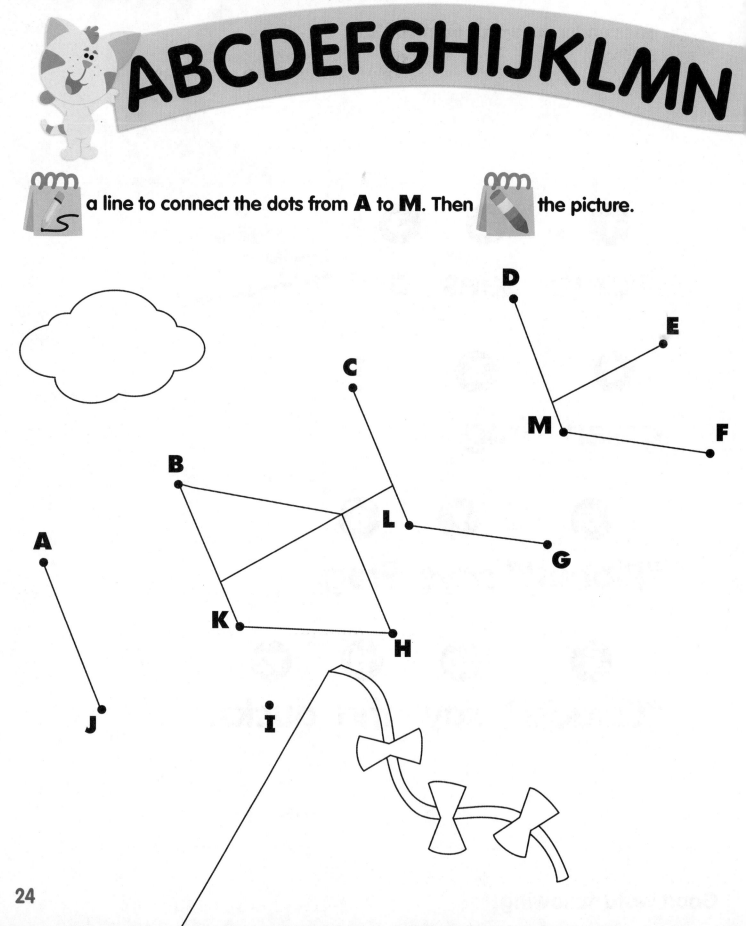

OPQRSTUVWXYZ

a line to connect the dots from **N** to **Z**. Then the picture.

Good job! Now the sky **blue**.

Periwinkle made up a game for Blue! Will you play, too?

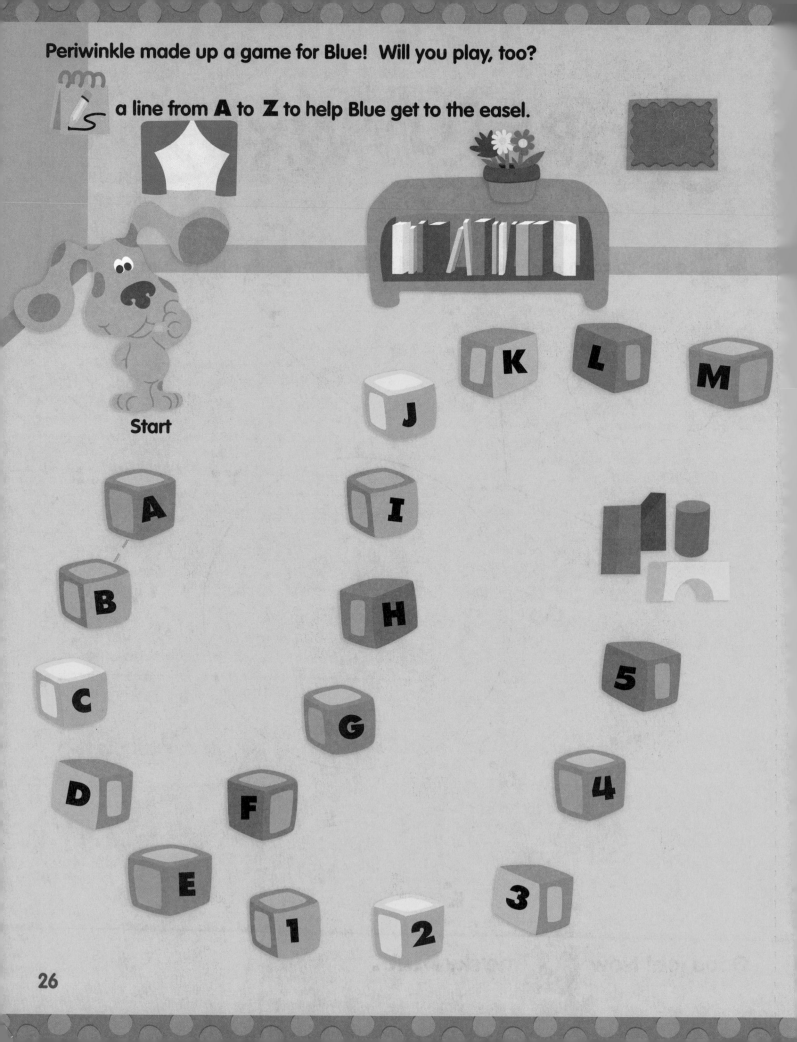 a line from **A** to **Z** to help Blue get to the easel.

Start

A B C D E F G H I J K L M

1 2 3 4 5

Finish

Blue wants to make a storybook!
Will you help?
Here's what to do:

Help your child make this cut-out storybook and practice the skills learned in this book.

1) Cut out pages 29 – 32.
2) Show your child how to fold the pages in half to make a 4-leaf booklet.
3) If you wish, staple the pages in the fold to keep the pages together for your child.
4) Ask your child to color the pictures.
5) Point out the book cover, the book title and the picture on the cover.
6) Read the book aloud to your child, asking him or her to point to the words in reading progression, from left to right and top to bottom.
7) Help your child practice turning the pages of the book. Ask, "Where is the first page?" and "Can you turn to the last page?"
8) Reinforce these pre-reading skills using other storybooks or board books.
9) If a storybook or board book includes the author's name and the illustrator's name on the cover, point these names out to your child. Explain that the author is the person who wrote the story and the illustrator is the person who drew the pictures.
10) Make sure to congratulate your child on what he or she has learned!

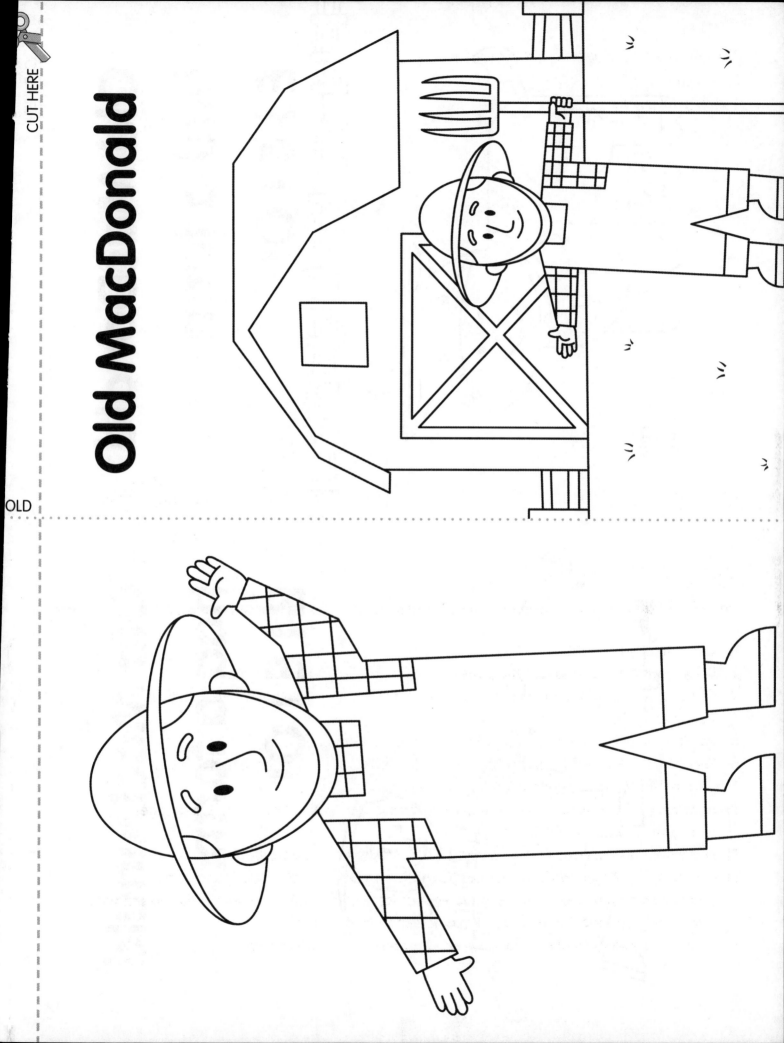

Old MacDonald

OLD

Old MacDonald
had a farm.
E I E I O!

1

FOLD

Old MacDonald
had a farm.
E I E I O!

6

2

Here an "oink."
There an "oink."
Everywhere an
"oink, oink!"

5

On that farm he
had a pig.
E I E I O!

With an "oink, oink"
here and an "oink,
oink" there.

3

FC

"oink, oink"

4